Weber Liquid Propane Grill Cookbook

The Ultimate Guide to Master Your Weber Grill with Flavorful Recipes and Step-by-Step Techniques for Beginners and Advanced Users

Mellsa H. Jones

© Copyright 2021 Mellsa H. Jones - All Rights Reserved.

In no way is it legal to reproduce, duplicate, or transmit any part of this document by either electronic means or in printed format. Recording of this publication is strictly prohibited, and any storage of this material is not allowed unless with written permission from the publisher. All rights reserved.

The information provided herein is stated to be truthful and consistent, in that any liability, regarding inattention or otherwise, by any usage or abuse of any policies, processes, or directions contained within is the solitary and complete responsibility of the recipient reader. Under no circumstances will any legal liability or blame be held against the publisher for any reparation, damages, or monetary loss due to the information herein, either directly or indirectly.

Respective authors own all copyrights not held by the publisher.

Legal Notice:

This book is copyright protected. This is only for personal use. You cannot amend, distribute, sell, use, quote or paraphrase any part of the content within this book without the consent of the author or copyright owner. Legal action will be pursued if this is breached.

Disclaimer Notice:

Please note the information contained within this document is for educational and entertainment purposes only. Every attempt has been made to provide accurate, up-to-date and reliable, complete information. No warranties of any kind are expressed or implied. Readers acknowledge that the author is not engaging in the rendering of legal, financial, medical or professional advice.

By reading this document, the reader agrees that under no circumstances are we responsible for any losses, direct or indirect, which are incurred as a result of the use of information contained within this document, including, but not limited to, errors, omissions, or inaccuracies.

Table of Contents

Introduction 6
Chapter 1: The Basics of Weber Liquid Propane Grill 7
    What is Weber Liquid Propane Grill? 7
    Features of Weber Liquid Propane Grill 7
    Grilling Tools and Accessories 9
    How does Weber Liquid Propane Grill Work? 9
    Tips and Tricks for Successful Grilling 10
    Cleaning and Maintenance 11
Chapter 2: Poultry 13
    Flavorful Pineapple Chicken 13
    Thai Chicken 14
    Simple Herb Chicken Breasts 15
    Lebanese Chicken Skewers 16
    Sweet & Spicy Chicken 17
    Peri Peri Chicken 18
    Marinated Greek Chicken 19
    Sweet & Spicy Chipotle Chicken 20
    Chicken Pineapple Kebabs 22
    Tandoori Chicken Skewers 23
    Quick & Easy Italian Chicken 24
    Jerk Chicken 25
    Honey Mustard Chicken 26
    Juicy Lemon Pepper Chicken 27
    Greek BBQ Chicken 28
    Blackened Chicken 29
    Chicken Burger Patties 30
    Paprika Lime Chicken Tenderloins 31
    Honey Herb Chicken Tenders 32
    Orange Chicken Skewers 33
Chapter 3: Beef, Pork & Lamb 34
    Delicious Short Ribs 34

Flavorful Beef Tenderloin 35
Tender Honey Mustard Pork Chops 36
Grill Steaks 37
Grill Rib-eye Steak 38
Herb Chuck Eye Steaks 39
Marinated Steak Skewers 40
Mustard Pork Chops 41
Bourbon Pork Tenderloin 42
Juicy Pork Skewers 43
Delicious Pork Patties 44
Lamb Loin Chops 45
Greek Lamb Chops 46
Classic Beef Patties 47
Flavorful Lamb Chops 48
Tandoori Lamb Chops 49
Herb Lamb Skewers 50
Tasty Lamb Patties 51
Quick & Easy Beef Patties 52
Greek Lamb Patties 53

Chapter 4: Fish & Seafood 54

Healthy Salmon Patties 54
Lemon Pepper Salmon 55
Grilled Mahi Mahi 56
Blackened White Fish 57
Tasty Fish Skewers 58
Spicy Salmon Fillets 59
Spicy White Fillets 60
Greek Fish Fillets 61
Asian Fish Fillets 62
Quick Shrimp Skewers 63
Lime Butter Fish Fillets 64
Delicious Swordfish 65
Marinated Shrimp Skewers 66

  Easy Grill Scallops.. 67

  Blackened Haddock... 68

Chapter 5: Vegetables & Side Dishes 69

  Perfect Brussels Sprouts 69

  Tender Asparagus 70

  Grill Garlic Zucchini 71

  Flavorful Grill Eggplant 72

  Simple Grill Sweet Potatoes 73

  Balsamic Vegetables 74

  Grill Mushrooms & Zucchini 75

  Grill Carrots 76

  Grill Tomatoes 77

  Grill Avocado 78

Chapter 6: Snacks 79

  Chili Lime Shrimp Skewers 79

  Tofu Steaks 80

  Pineapple Shrimp Skewers 81

  Spicy Tofu Skewers 82

  Mushroom Skewers 83

  Pineapple Chicken Skewers 84

  Hawaiian Chicken Skewers 85

  Simple Chicken Skewers 86

  Mexican Grill Shrimp 87

  Grill Pork Patties 88

Chapter 7: Desserts 89

  Delicious Grill Pineapple 89

  Grill Apple Slices 90

  Grilled Peaches 91

  Grill Pears 92

  Fruit Skewers 93

Conclusion 94

Introduction

The Weber Spirit II is one of the innovative and advanced gas grills works on liquid propane gas. The grill comes with compact size and made up from stainless steel material. If you enjoy your weekends and holidays cooking outdoor food on regular basis then Weber spirit II gas grill is one of the best options available in the market which fulfils your outdoor cooking needs. The Weber spirit models come with Flavorizer bars to catch the drippings and create smoke to add the smoky flavour into your food it also protects burners from dripping to avoid clogs. The grill comes with a bigger cooking surface area and it is capable to grill 4 to 5 people's food into the single cooking cycle.

The Weber Spirit II grill comes with three individual gas controller knobs allows you to create direct heat and indirect heat areas to cook your food. The grill also packed with smart features like iGill controller and GS4 grilling system. The Weber Spirit II model comes with fuel tank scale. You just need to mount the propane tank over the scale and some indicator sign helps you to know the gas level in the propane tank. The grill comes with 10 years of warranty from the date of purchase.

This cookbook contains 80 healthy and tasty recipes comes from different categories like poultry, beef, pork, lamb, seafood, fish, side dishes, vegetables, snacks, and desserts. The recipes written in this book are unique and written into an easily understandable form. All the recipes start with their preparation and cooking time followed by step by step cooking instructions. In the end, each recipe ends with their nutritional value information. The nutritional value information will help to keep track of daily calories intake. We are proud to announce that this is one of the first book available in the market on this topic thanks for choosing my cookbook. The information given in this book will help you with your outdoor cooking. I hope you love and enjoy all the healthy and delicious recipes written in this cookbook.

Chapter 1: The Basics of Weber Liquid Propane Grill

What is Weber Liquid Propane Grill?

Weber liquid propane grill is one of the advanced and compact size grills works on liquid propane. The structure of the grill is sturdy and made up of stainless steel material. The grill equipped with three stainless steel burners with separate controller system. The separate controller knob allows you to operate each burner individually to form direct and indirect heat zones. The burners are arranged such a way to cover all the cooking surface area equally so you will get even cooking results. A single burner produces 10000 BTU/hour heat and together three burners are capable to produce 30000 BTU/hour heat. The grill comes with side tables used for placing ingredients, serving plates and cooking utensils. The left side table of the grill is foldable. The grill unit has two large heavy-duty plastic wheel which helps to move grill over grass and uneven surface easily while carrying from one place to another place.

The Weber grill has loaded with advanced features like GS4 grilling system, iGrill capability and other features like infinity ignition, easy grease management system, porcelain coated reversible grill grate etc. The iGrill feature allows you to monitor the internal temperature of the food with the help of mobile device connected with iGrill through wireless. The bottom side open cart design shelf allows storing and accessing your cooking accessories easily. The easily removable grease tray makes your cleaning process faster. Due to its large grilling surface area, it allows you to cook 3 to 4 family members' food in a single cooking cycle. The grill also having a propane tank scale tools which helps you to know how much gas is left in the tank.

Features of Weber Liquid Propane Grill

The Weber liquid propane grill is loaded with various kinds of features these features include.

1. **GS4 grilling system:** The GS4 grilling system improves your backyard grilling skills. The system works on 4 components like *Infinity crossover ignition* ensures to ignite whenever you light up it first time or every time. *Burners* the 3 burners made up from stainless steel material helps to evenly distribute the heat over cooking

grates. *Flavorizer bar* protects burners from dripping oil and liquid from the food it vaporised drips while extra drip from food is collected by the grease management system. *The grease management system* allows collecting the un-vaporised drip oils and liquid into the removable tray which is situated exactly under the cook-box.

2. **IGrill 3:** This is one of the smart function in which you can easily monitor the internal food temperature while cooking your food. To work this on your mobile you need to download the Weber grill app and then connect your mobile through the device by Bluetooth. It allows you to run 4 thermometer probes while grilling your food.

3. **Built-in thermometer:** The built-in thermometer allows you to know the internal temperature of the grill. So you can adjust the internal grill temperature by adjusting the burner flame.

4. **Warming rack:** The warming rack is exactly situated over the main grill grate. It is used to toast your favourite burger buns and also help to keep your food warm. The food placed over warming rack cooks slowly at low temperature.

5. **Porcelain-coated grate:** The Double-sided reversible porcelain-coated cast iron grill grates allow you to cook a variety of foods. The thin side of the grill grate is used while cooking delicate food like shrimp, fish etc. The other thick side creates sear marks on your food and also improve the flavours into your food.

6. **Side tables with tool hooks:** Side tables are used to hold the ingredients, utensils, grilling tools and more. You can hang the grilling tools with the help of hooks. The left side table is easily folded down while storing your grill in less space.

7. **Fuel Gauge:** The fuel gauge is one of the best parts allows you to know the rough idea about propane tank level. You will also get an idea of how much fuel you need to cook your food every time.

8. **Easily accessible gas tank:** The gas tank of the grill is situated at the outside so you can easily access gas tank for refilling.

9. **Open bottom cart:** The open cart space is situated at the bottom side of the grill. The open cart is designed to give you extra space to your accessories and cooking utensils.

Grilling Tools and Accessories

The right grilling tool is necessary to make you a master chief into outdoor grilling. Some of the necessary accessories and tools are given as follows.

1. **IGrill and thermometers:** The Weber iGrill tool is mounted on your spirit 2 grill. The tool is connected to your mobile with the help of the iGrill 3 apps and Bluetooth. It monitors the four cuts of meats at a time and notifies you the internal temperature of the food reaches its perfect doneness position.
2. **Heat resistant gloves:** While grilling your food you must wear heat resistant gloves to protect your hand from a hot surface, splatter or check your meat. The best choice is used silicon gloves which gives better grip and allow you to handle juicy meats, hot grates and everything directly with your hand.
3. **Heavy Duty Grilling Tongs:** The heavy-duty grilling tongs are made up from stainless steel material used to flip, grip, and lift the large piece of meats easily. There are various kinds of tongs used while grilling choose tongs as per your cooking needs. A heavy-duty shark tong is one of the best tongs keep your hand at a safe distance from the hot cooking surface area.
4. **Veggie Basket:** The grilling veggie basket is used to cook your veggies quickly and evenly by just giving one toss. It helps to cook small pieces of different vegetables and also prevent the vegetable pieces from falling over grill grate.
5. **Basting Brush:** It is used to spread the butter, marinades, sausage, oil or glaze over food. The brush made up from heat resistant silicone bristle comes with plastic handle for easy grip.
6. **Grill brush:** Grill brush is one of the essential tools that help to clean the grate surface area for dry food, debris between grates. Stainless steel bristle grilling brush is used to clean Weber grill grates.

How does Weber Liquid Propane Grill Work?

The Weber liquid propane grill is easy to operate you just need to follow the step by step instructions given below.

1. Before starting your grill make sure propane gas cylinder is fixed its position and connected properly with Weber grill.

2. Now open the lid and check the gill burner control knob is set at *OFF* position. Then turn on the tank valve by turning slowly at anticlockwise and wait for 1 minute to pass the gas from the gas hose.
3. Now push the gas controller knob 1 and move it anticlockwise direction to set it on *Start/High* position.
4. Immediately push and hold the ignition system button till you have heard the sound like ticking. Now check the burners lit properly by looking through grill grates.
5. Remaining 2 burners are lit from burner 1 so just push the controller knob and turn anticlockwise position and set it on *Start/High* position.
6. Now close the lid and preheat the grill at 3 burners on at *Start/High* position for 10 to 15 minutes or the thermometer reaches 500°F temperature.
7. Now your grill is ready. Open the lid and place your food inside close the lid and adjust the temperature knob in between High-medium-low settings as per your recipe needs.
8. To check the internal temperature of large meat cuts you can use grill accessories which allow you to monitor your food doneness on your mobile device through Bluetooth connectivity.
9. When the internal temperature reaches its doneness point then your food is cooked and ready for serve. Now turn off the entire burner controller knob and remove your food of serving.

Tips and Tricks for Successful Grilling

The following tips and tricks will make your grilling process faster and easy.

- **Don't forget to preheat your grill every time:** Before placing your food for grilling always preheat your grill at its highest settings until the thermometer reaches 500° F temperature. If the grill is not preheated then there are chances to stick your food over the grate.
- **Be ready with your ingredients:** Before starting the actual cooking process make sure all the necessary ingredients and essential tools are ready and within your arms reach. If you never prepare your food and ingredients then there are chances to burn your food to run back in the kitchen and finding your ingredients.

- **Always use clean grate:** Placing your food on a dirty grill gate is not a good idea. When the grill grate is preheated then with the help of stainless steel bristle grill brush are used to clean the grill grate surface.
- **Don't overcrowd food on a griddle:** The over crowd food on the grill grates gives uneven cooking results. If you want even and faster-cooking results then keep at least 30 % space in between two pieces of the food. This will help to move or flip the large pieces of meat or food easily.
- **Monitor Food internal temperature:** You can monitor the internal temperature of the food by using iGrill wireless monitoring equipment. It is capable to measure 4 piece temperature at a time. This will help you to know the food doneness.
- **Use proper tools and accessories:** Always make sure before grilling your food you have all necessary tools and accessories like grilling tongs, safety gloves, basting brush, grill brush and thermometers are available. These tools make your cooking process faster and easy.

Cleaning and Maintenance

Cleaning is one of the important processes done after every use of the grill. It will help to increase the lifespan of equipment and also gives clean cooking environments. Just follow the simple cleaning instruction given below to clean your grill properly.

1. **Cleaning the lid**

Due to regular use grease and smokes are converted into carbon and this carbon is deposited on the inner surface of the lid.

Use stainless steel bristle grill brush to remove the carbon and then wipe out the inner surface of the lid with the help of a paper towel when the grill is warm.

2. **Cleaning cooking grates**

Clean grate surface for derbies stuck between the grates with the help of stainless steel bristle grill brush.

Turn the grate and again repeat this process and remove the grates and place it aside.

3. **Cleaning Flavorizer bars**

Flavorizer bars are catch drippings from your food and create smoke to add flavours into your food. It also protects the burners to clog.

Use a plastic scraper to scrap the Flavorizer bar. If necessary you can also use a stainless steel bristle brush to clean the bars.

After cleaning the bars remove and place it aside.

4. Cleaning Burners

Clean the burners carefully with the help of stainless steel bristle grill brush.

Make sure the ignition electrode is safe while cleaning burners.

5. Clean grease management system

Just swipe out the dripping pan and remove the disposable foil pan and set new foil pan into dripping pan.

The design of the grease management system is simple and you can easily remove and clean the components.

6. Clean outside of the grill

Wipe the outer surface of the grill with the help of warm soapy water.

Do not use any harsh chemicals to clean the outer surface of the grill.

Now assemble all the parts to its original position. Your grill is now ready for the next use.

Chapter 2: Poultry

Flavorful Pineapple Chicken

Preparation Time: 10 minutes
Cooking Time: 15 minutes
Serve: 4

Ingredients:

- 4 chicken breasts, boneless
- 1 ½ tbsp Worcestershire sauce
- 1 tbsp garlic, minced
- ½ cup BBQ sauce
- ¾ cup pineapple juice
- ¾ cup Bourbon

Directions:

1. Add chicken breasts into the zip-lock bag.
2. Mix remaining ingredients and pour over chicken. Seal bag and place in the refrigerator for overnight.
3. Preheat the grill over medium heat.
4. Remove chicken from marinade and place on grill and cook for 12-15 minutes or until internal temperature reaches 165 F.
5. Serve and enjoy.

Nutritional Value (Amount per Serving):

- Calories 454
- Fat 11 g
- Carbohydrates 19.2 g
- Sugar 14 g
- Protein 42.5 g
- Cholesterol 130 mg

Thai Chicken

Preparation Time: 10 minutes
Cooking Time: 6 minutes
Serve: 5

Ingredients:

- 2 lbs chicken thighs, boneless & skinless
- 2 tbsp honey
- 3 tbsp brown sugar
- 1 tsp sesame oil
- 2 tbsp sherry wine
- 3 tbsp fish sauce
- 2 tsp red chili, chopped
- 2 tbsp fresh lime juice
- 1 ½ tbsp garlic, minced
- 1 lemongrass stalk, chopped
- ½ tsp pepper

Directions:

1. Add chicken and remaining ingredients into the zip-lock bag. Seal bag and place in the refrigerator for overnight.
2. Preheat the grill over high heat.
3. Remove chicken thighs from marinade and place on grill and cook for 3 minutes on each side.
4. Serve and enjoy.

Nutritional Value (Amount per Serving):

- Calories 418
- Fat 14.4 g
- Carbohydrates 15.7 g
- Sugar 13 g
- Protein 53.4 g
- Cholesterol 161 mg

Simple Herb Chicken Breasts

Preparation Time: 10 minutes
Cooking Time: 10 minutes
Serve: 4

Ingredients:

- 1 ½ lbs chicken breasts, skinless
- 3 tbsp fresh lemon juice
- ¼ tsp rosemary, chopped
- ½ tsp oregano, chopped
- ½ tsp thyme, chopped
- 2 tbsp parsley, chopped
- 1 tbsp garlic, minced
- 1/3 cup olive oil
- ½ tsp salt

Directions:

1. Add chicken and remaining ingredients into the zip-lock bag. Seal bag and place in the refrigerator for 4 hours.
2. Preheat the grill over medium heat.
3. Place marinated chicken on the grill and cook for 5 minutes, flip chicken and cook for 5 minutes more or until internal temperature reaches to 160 F.
4. Serve and enjoy.

Nutritional Value (Amount per Serving):

- Calories 475
- Fat 29.6 g
- Carbohydrates 1.3 g
- Sugar 0.3 g
- Protein 49.5 g
- Cholesterol 151 mg

Lebanese Chicken Skewers

Preparation Time: 10 minutes
Cooking Time: 16 minutes
Serve: 6

Ingredients:

- 2 lbs chicken breasts, boneless & cut into pieces
- ½ tsp ground ginger
- ½ tsp oregano
- ½ tsp cinnamon
- 1 tsp paprika
- 1 tbsp tomato paste
- 1 tbsp garlic, minced
- ¼ cup olive oil
- ¼ cup fresh lemon juice
- ½ cup yogurt
- ¼ tsp pepper
- 1 tsp salt

Directions:

1. Add chicken and remaining ingredients into the large mixing bowl and mix well. Cover and place in the refrigerator for 4 hours.
2. Thread marinated chicken onto the skewers.
3. Preheat the grill over medium heat.
4. Place chicken skewers on the grill and cook for 5-8 minutes on each side.
5. Serve and enjoy.

Nutritional Value (Amount per Serving):

- Calories 383
- Fat 20 g
- Carbohydrates 3.2 g
- Sugar 2.1 g
- Protein 45.3 g
- Cholesterol 136 mg

Sweet & Spicy Chicken

Preparation Time: 10 minutes
Cooking Time: 14 minutes
Serve: 6

Ingredients:

- 2 lbs chicken thighs, boneless & skinless
- 1 tbsp garlic, minced
- 1 tbsp ginger, grated
- 1 ½ tbsp rice wine
- 2 tbsp sesame oil
- 2 tbsp brown sugar
- ¼ cup honey
- 3 tbsp gochujang
- ½ cup soy sauce

Directions:

1. Add chicken and remaining ingredients into the zip-lock bag. Seal bag and place in the refrigerator for 8 hours.
2. Preheat the grill over medium heat.
3. Place chicken on the grill and cook for 5-7 minutes on each side or until internal temperature reaches 165 F.
4. Serve and enjoy.

Nutritional Value (Amount per Serving):

- Calories 427
- Fat 15.8 g
- Carbohydrates 24.1 g
- Sugar 18.9 g
- Protein 45.8 g
- Cholesterol 135 mg

Peri Peri Chicken

Preparation Time: 10 minutes
Cooking Time: 20 minutes
Serve: 6

Ingredients:

- 6 chicken drumsticks
- ½ cup olive oil
- 1 tbsp oregano
- 2 tbsp vinegar
- 1 tsp ground black pepper
- 2 tbsp paprika
- 5 garlic cloves
- 6 red chilies
- 1 red bell pepper, diced
- Salt

Directions:

1. Add all ingredients except chicken into the blender and blend until smooth.
2. Add chicken and blended mixture into the mixing bowl and mix well. Cover and place in the refrigerator for 4 hours.
3. Preheat the grill over medium heat.
4. Place chicken on the grill and cook for 7-10 minutes then flip chicken and cook for 7-10 minutes more.
5. Serve and enjoy.

Nutritional Value (Amount per Serving):

- Calories 244
- Fat 19.9 g
- Carbohydrates 4.7 g
- Sugar 1.5 g
- Protein 13.5 g
- Cholesterol 40 mg

Marinated Greek Chicken

Preparation Time: 10 minutes
Cooking Time: 14 minutes
Serve: 4

Ingredients:

- 4 chicken breasts, boneless & skinless
- ½ tsp paprika
- 1 tsp dried parsley
- 1 tsp dried thyme
- 1 tsp dried rosemary
- 1 tbsp dried oregano
- 1 ½ tsp ginger garlic paste
- ¼ cup fresh lemon juice
- ¼ cup olive oil
- Pepper
- Salt

Directions:

1. Add chicken and remaining ingredients into the zip-lock bag. Seal bag and place in the refrigerator for 8 hours.
2. Preheat the grill over medium heat.
3. Place chicken on the grill and cook for 5-7 minutes, flip chicken and cook for 5-7 minutes more or until cooked through.
4. Serve and enjoy.

Nutritional Value (Amount per Serving):

- Calories 405
- Fat 24.1 g
- Carbohydrates 2.7 g
- Sugar 0.4 g
- Protein 42.9 g
- Cholesterol 130 mg

Sweet & Spicy Chipotle Chicken

Preparation Time: 10 minutes
Cooking Time: 14 minutes
Serve: 4

Ingredients:

- 4 chicken breasts, boneless
- For marinade:
- 1 tbsp water
- ¼ cup cilantro
- ¼ tsp cumin
- 2 lime juice
- 5 garlic cloves
- 2 tbsp honey
- 1 tbsp olive oil
- 7 oz chipotle peppers in adobo sauce
- ¼ tsp pepper
- ¼ tsp salt

Directions:

1. Add marinade ingredients into the blender and blend until smooth.
2. Add chicken and blended mixture into the zip-lock bag. Seal bag and place in the refrigerator for 4 hours.
3. Preheat the grill over medium heat.
4. Place marinated chicken on the grill and cook for 5-7 minutes on each side or until internal temperature reaches 165 F.
5. Serve and enjoy.

Nutritional Value (Amount per Serving):

- Calories 375
- Fat 16.4 g
- Carbohydrates 13.9 g

- Sugar 9 g
- Protein 44.6 g
- Cholesterol 140 mg

Chicken Pineapple Kebabs

Preparation Time: 10 minutes
Cooking Time: 10 minutes
Serve: 6

Ingredients:

- 3 ½ lbs chicken thighs, boneless & cut into pieces
- 1 pineapple, cut into chunks
- For marinade:
- 1 ½ tbsp brown sugar
- 2 tbsp vinegar
- 1 small onion, minced
- 5 garlic cloves, minced
- ½ cup soy sauce
- 1 cup pineapple juice

Directions:

1. Add all marinade ingredients into the large mixing bowl and mix well. Add chicken and pineapple pieces into the bowl and mix well. Cover and place in the refrigerator overnight.
2. Thread marinated chicken and pineapple pieces onto the skewers.
3. Preheat the grill over medium heat.
4. Place chicken skewers on grill and cook for 5 minutes on each side or until internal temperature reaches 165 F.
5. Serve and enjoy.

Nutritional Value (Amount per Serving):

- Calories 568
- Fat 19.7 g
- Carbohydrates 14.8 g
- Sugar 10 g
- Protein 78.5 g
- Cholesterol 235 mg

Tandoori Chicken Skewers

Preparation Time: 10 minutes
Cooking Time: 12 minutes
Serve: 6

Ingredients:

- 2 lbs chicken thighs, boneless & cut into pieces
- ½ tsp pepper
- 1 tsp olive oil
- 1 red bell pepper, cut into pieces
- ¼ onion, cut into pieces
- ½ tsp garlic powder
- ¼ cup curry paste
- 1 ½ tbsp lemon juice
- 1 ½ cups Greek yogurt
- ¾ tsp kosher salt

Directions:

1. Add yogurt, lemon juice, curry paste, garlic powder, oil, pepper, and salt into the large bowl and mix well. Add chicken and mix well. Cover and place in the refrigerator for 8 hours.
2. Thread marinated chicken, bell pepper, and onion onto the skewers.
3. Preheat the grill over medium heat.
4. Place chicken skewers on grill and cook for 6 minutes on each side or until cooked through.
5. Serve and enjoy.

Nutritional Value (Amount per Serving):

- Calories 409
- Fat 18.9 g
- Carbohydrates 7.2 g
- Sugar 3.4 g
- Protein 49.6 g
- Cholesterol 137 mg

Quick & Easy Italian Chicken

Preparation Time: 10 minutes
Cooking Time: 10 minutes
Serve: 4

Ingredients:

- 4 chicken breasts, boneless
- ¾ cup Italian dressing

Directions:

1. Add chicken and Italian dressing into the zip-lock bag. Seal bag and place in the refrigerator for 12 hours.
2. Preheat the grill over medium heat.
3. Place chicken on the grill and cook for 5 minutes, flip chicken and cook for 5 minutes more or until internal temperature reaches to 165 F.
4. Serve and enjoy.

Nutritional Value (Amount per Serving):

- Calories 406
- Fat 23.3 g
- Carbohydrates 4.6 g
- Sugar 3.7 g
- Protein 42.4 g
- Cholesterol 159 mg

Jerk Chicken

Preparation Time: 10 minutes
Cooking Time: 10 minutes
Serve: 6

Ingredients:

- 2 lbs chicken breasts, boneless
- 1 lime juice
- 1 lime zest
- 1 tsp all-spice
- 1 tsp cinnamon
- 1 tsp cayenne
- 1 tbsp smoked paprika
- 3 tbsp thyme
- 1 tbsp garlic, minced
- 2 tbsp olive oil
- Pepper
- Salt

Directions:

1. Add chicken and remaining ingredients into the zip-lock bag. Seal bag and place in the refrigerator for overnight.
2. Preheat the grill over medium heat.
3. Place chicken on the grill and cook for 5 minutes on each side or until cooked through.
4. Serve and enjoy.

Nutritional Value (Amount per Serving):

- Calories 341
- Fat 16.2 g
- Carbohydrates 3.2 g
- Sugar 0.4 g
- Protein 44.2 g
- Cholesterol 135 mg

Honey Mustard Chicken

Preparation Time: 10 minutes
Cooking Time: 8 minutes
Serve: 4

Ingredients:

- 4 chicken breasts, boneless
- 2 tsp lemon juice
- 1 tbsp olive oil
- ¼ cup Dijon mustard
- ¼ cup honey
- 2 tbsp butter, melted
- Pepper
- Salt

Directions:

1. Add chicken and remaining ingredients into the large bowl and mix well.
2. Preheat the grill over medium heat.
3. Place chicken on the grill and cook for 5 minutes, flip chicken and cook for 5 minutes more or until cooked through.
4. Serve and enjoy.

Nutritional Value (Amount per Serving):

- Calories 156
- Fat 20.7 g
- Carbohydrates 18.4 g
- Sugar 17.6 g
- Protein 43.1 g
- Cholesterol 145 mg

Juicy Lemon Pepper Chicken

Preparation Time: 10 minutes
Cooking Time: 16 minutes
Serve: 6

Ingredients:

- 6 chicken breasts, boneless
- 2 tbsp lemon pepper seasoning
- 2 tbsp Worcestershire sauce
- 1 cup fresh lemon juice
- ½ cup olive oil
- ½ tsp salt

Directions:

1. Add lemon juice, oil, Worcestershire sauce, lemon pepper seasoning, and salt into the large bowl and mix well.
2. Add chicken into the bowl and mix well and place in the refrigerator for 1 hour.
3. Preheat the grill over medium heat.
4. Place chicken on the grill and cook for 8 minutes, flip chicken and cook for 8 minutes more or until cooked through.
5. Serve and enjoy.

Nutritional Value (Amount per Serving):

- Calories 442
- Fat 28 g
- Carbohydrates 3.2 g
- Sugar 1.9 g
- Protein 42.8 g
- Cholesterol 130 mg

Greek BBQ Chicken

Preparation Time: 10 minutes
Cooking Time: 12 minutes
Serve: 6

Ingredients:

- 6 chicken breasts, boneless
- 1 tbsp red chili flakes
- 1 tbsp chili powder
- ¾ cup Italian dressing
- ½ cup BBQ sauce

Directions:

1. Add chicken, chili flakes, chili powder, Italian dressing, and BBQ sauce into the zip-lock bag. Seal bag and place in the refrigerator for overnight.
2. Preheat the grill over medium heat.
3. Place marinated chicken on the grill and cook for 6 minutes on each side or until cooked through.
4. Serve and enjoy.

Nutritional Value (Amount per Serving):

- Calories 398
- Fat 19.4 g
- Carbohydrates 11.3 g
- Sugar 8 g
- Protein 42.5 g
- Cholesterol 150 mg

Blackened Chicken

Preparation Time: 10 minutes
Cooking Time: 10 minutes
Serve: 4

Ingredients:

- 1 lb chicken breast, boneless
- ¼ tsp pepper
- ¼ tsp garlic powder
- ¼ tsp onion powder
- ¼ tsp chili powder
- 1 tsp Italian seasoning
- 1 tbsp paprika
- ¼ tsp garlic salt

Directions:

1. Add chicken, pepper, garlic powder, onion powder, chili powder, Italian seasoning, paprika, and salt into the mixing bowl and mix well.
2. Preheat the grill over high heat.
3. Place chicken on the grill and cook for 5 minutes on each side or until internal temperature reaches 165 F.
4. Serve and enjoy.

Nutritional Value (Amount per Serving):

- Calories 140
- Fat 3.4 g
- Carbohydrates 1.6 g
- Sugar 0.4 g
- Protein 24.4 g
- Cholesterol 73 mg

Chicken Burger Patties

Preparation Time: 10 minutes
Cooking Time: 12 minutes
Serve: 6

Ingredients:

- 1 lb ground chicken
- 1 tsp cumin powder
- ½ tsp cayenne pepper
- 1 ½ tbsp chili powder
- ½ bell pepper, diced
- 1 small onion, diced
- ½ cup tortilla chips, baked & crushed
- Salt

Directions:

1. Add all ingredients into the bowl and mix until well combined.
2. Preheat the grill over medium heat.
3. Make patties from the mixture and spray with cooking spray.
4. Place chicken patties on the grill and cook for 5-6 minutes on each side or until cooked through.
5. Serve and enjoy.

Nutritional Value (Amount per Serving):

- Calories 159
- Fat 6.1 g
- Carbohydrates 4 g
- Sugar 1.2 g
- Protein 22.5 g
- Cholesterol 67 mg

Paprika Lime Chicken Tenderloins

Preparation Time: 10 minutes
Cooking Time: 6 minutes
Serve: 2

Ingredients:

- 6 chicken tenderloins
- 1 tbsp olive oil
- 1 tbsp lime juice
- ½ tsp pepper
- ½ tsp ground coriander
- ½ tsp allspice
- ½ tsp cayenne
- 2 tsp paprika
- ½ tsp garlic, minced
- 1 tsp salt

Directions:

1. Add chicken and remaining ingredients into the zip-lock bag, seal bag, and place in the refrigerator for 1 hour.
2. Preheat the grill over medium heat.
3. Place chicken tenders on the grill and cook for 3 minutes on each side or until cooked through.
4. Serve and enjoy.

Nutritional Value (Amount per Serving):

- Calories 341
- Fat 10.4 g
- Carbohydrates 5.4 g
- Sugar 0.3 g
- Protein 54.5 g
- Cholesterol 135 mg

Honey Herb Chicken Tenders

Preparation Time: 10 minutes
Cooking Time: 10 minutes
Serve: 4

Ingredients:

- 1 ½ lbs chicken tenderloins
- 1 tsp dried oregano
- 1 tsp dried rosemary
- 2 tbsp herb de Provence
- 2 tbsp lemon juice
- 2 tbsp olive oil
- ¼ cup honey
- 1 shallot, minced
- 1/3 cup Dijon mustard
- Pepper
- Salt

Directions:

1. Add chicken tenderloins and remaining ingredients into the mixing bowl and mix well. Cover and place in the refrigerator overnight.
2. Preheat the grill over medium heat.
3. Place chicken on the grill and cook for 5 minutes on each side or until internal temperature reaches 165 F.
4. Serve and enjoy.

Nutritional Value (Amount per Serving):

- Calories 178
- Fat 8.4 g
- Carbohydrates 20 g
- Sugar 17.8 g
- Protein 7.9 g
- Cholesterol 17 mg

Orange Chicken Skewers

Preparation Time: 10 minutes
Cooking Time: 20 minutes
Serve: 6

Ingredients:

- 3 chicken breasts, boneless & cut into pieces
- ½ tbsp cornstarch
- 1 tsp pepper
- 1 tbsp garlic, minced
- 1 tbsp olive oil
- 1 tbsp orange zest
- ¼ cup orange juice
- ¼ cup soy sauce

Directions:

1. Add chicken and remaining ingredients into the zip-lock bag, seal bag, and place in the refrigerator for overnight.
2. Preheat the grill over medium heat.
3. Thread marinated chicken onto the skewers.
4. Place chicken skewers on grill and cook for 8-10 minutes on each side or until internal temperature reaches 165 F.
5. Serve and enjoy.

Nutritional Value (Amount per Serving):

- Calories 176
- Fat 7.8 g
- Carbohydrates 3.4 g
- Sugar 1.1 g
- Protein 22 g
- Cholesterol 65 mg

Chapter 3: Beef, Pork & Lamb

Delicious Short Ribs

Preparation Time: 10 minutes
Cooking Time: 12 minutes
Serve: 4

Ingredients:

- 2 lbs beef short ribs
- For marinade:
- 1 green onion, chopped
- ½ tbsp sesame seeds, toasted
- 1 tbsp sesame oil
- 1 tbsp garlic, minced
- 2 tbsp chili paste
- 3 tbsp brown sugar
- ½ cup mirin
- ½ cup soy sauce

Directions:

1. Add beef ribs and marinade ingredients into the zip-lock bag. Seal bag and place in the refrigerator for overnight.
2. Preheat the grill over high heat.
3. Place beef ribs on the grill and cook for 5-6 minutes on each side or until cooked through.
4. Serve and enjoy.

Nutritional Value (Amount per Serving):

- Calories 623
- Fat 25.7 g
- Carbohydrates 27.3 g
- Sugar 17.2 g
- Protein 68.4 g
- Cholesterol 209 mg

Flavorful Beef Tenderloin

Preparation Time: 10 minutes
Cooking Time: 30 minutes
Serve: 6

Ingredients:

- 2 lbs beef tenderloin
- 2 tbsp olive oil
- 2 tbsp balsamic vinegar
- For rub:
- ½ tsp cayenne
- ½ tsp garlic powder
- ¼ tsp pepper
- ½ tsp onion powder
- ¼ tsp paprika
- 1 tsp sea salt

Directions:

1. In a small bowl, mix together all rub ingredients and set them aside.
2. Brush beef tenderloin with oil and vinegar and rub with spice mixture.
3. Preheat the grill over high heat.
4. Place beef tenderloin on the grill and cook for 4 minutes on each side.
5. Turn heat to medium and cover and cook for 15-20 minutes more or until internal temperature reaches 135 F.
6. Slice and serve.

Nutritional Value (Amount per Serving):

- Calories 355
- Fat 18.5 g
- Carbohydrates 0.6 g
- Sugar 0.2 g
- Protein 43.9 g
- Cholesterol 139 mg

Tender Honey Mustard Pork Chops

Preparation Time: 10 minutes
Cooking Time: 8 minutes
Serve: 4

Ingredients:

- 4 pork chops, bone-in
- ¼ cup brown sugar
- ¼ tsp cayenne
- 1 tsp onion powder
- 3 tbsp mustard
- ½ cup honey
- ½ tsp cornstarch
- 2 tbsp apple cider vinegar
- Pepper
- Salt

Directions:

1. Add brown sugar, cayenne, onion powder, mustard, honey, cornstarch, and vinegar to the saucepan and cook for 5 minutes.
2. Preheat the grill over medium heat.
3. Season pork chops with pepper and salt and place on grill and cook for 3-4 minutes on each side or until cooked through.
4. Brush pork chops brown sugar mixture and serve.

Nutritional Value (Amount per Serving):

- Calories 464
- Fat 22.3 g
- Carbohydrates 47.7 g
- Sugar 44.4 g
- Protein 20.3 g
- Cholesterol 69 mg

Grill Steaks

Preparation Time: 10 minutes
Cooking Time: 10 minutes
Serve: 2

Ingredients:

- 24 oz New York strip steaks
- 2 tbsp olive oil
- 1 cup chermoula

Directions:

1. Add steaks, oil, and chermoula in a mixing bowl and mix well. Cover and place in the refrigerator for 1 hour.
2. Preheat the grill over medium heat.
3. Place steaks on the grill and cook for 4-5 minutes on each side or until internal temperature reaches 140 F.
4. Serve and enjoy.

Nutritional Value (Amount per Serving):

- Calories 149
- Fat 15.3 g
- Carbohydrates 0 g
- Sugar 0 g
- Protein 4.1 g
- Cholesterol 11 mg

Grill Rib-eye Steak

Preparation Time: 10 minutes
Cooking Time: 15 minutes
Serve: 6

Ingredients:

- 3 rib-eye steaks
- 1/3 cup olive oil
- 2 tsp pepper
- 3 tsp kosher salt

Directions:

1. Place steaks, oil, pepper, and salt into the large bowl and mix well. Cover and place in the refrigerator overnight.
2. Preheat the grill over medium heat.
3. Place steaks on the grill and cook for 4-5 minutes on each side or until internal temperature reaches 130 F.
4. Serve and enjoy.

Nutritional Value (Amount per Serving):

- Calories 303
- Fat 28.5 g
- Carbohydrates 0.5 g
- Sugar 0 g
- Protein 12.1 g
- Cholesterol 45 mg

Herb Chuck Eye Steaks

Preparation Time: 10 minutes
Cooking Time: 10 minutes
Serve: 4

Ingredients:

- 4 chuck eye steaks
- 2 tsp olive oil
- 1 tsp dry mustard
- 1 tsp pepper
- 2 tsp dried rosemary
- 4 tsp dried thyme
- 4 tsp dried oregano
- 2 tsp kosher salt

Directions:

1. Add steaks, oil, mustard, pepper, rosemary, thyme, oregano, and salt into the bowl and mix well. Cover and place in the refrigerator for 1 hour.
2. Place steaks on the grill and cook for 5 minutes on each side or until the internal temperature reaches 130 F.
3. Serve and enjoy.

Nutritional Value (Amount per Serving):

- Calories 285
- Fat 21.9 g
- Carbohydrates 2.6 g
- Sugar 0.1 g
- Protein 21.6 g
- Cholesterol 75 mg

Marinated Steak Skewers

Preparation Time: 10 minutes
Cooking Time: 8 minutes
Serve: 4

Ingredients:

- 2 lbs top sirloin steak, cut into cubes
- 1 tbsp garlic, minced
- 2 tbsp lemon juice
- 2 tbsp Worcestershire sauce
- 2 tbsp olive oil
- ¼ cup soy sauce
- ½ cup red wine

Directions:

1. Add steak cubes and remaining ingredients into the bowl and let it marinate for 2 hours.
2. Preheat the grill over medium heat.
3. Thread marinated steak cubes onto the skewers.
4. Place steak skewers on the grill and cook for 2 minutes on each side.
5. Serve and enjoy.

Nutritional Value (Amount per Serving):

- Calories 527
- Fat 21.2 g
- Carbohydrates 4.4 g
- Sugar 2.2 g
- Protein 70 g
- Cholesterol 203 mg

Mustard Pork Chops

Preparation Time: 10 minutes
Cooking Time: 10 minutes
Serve: 4

Ingredients:

- 4 pork chops
- 2 garlic cloves, minced
- 1 tbsp tamari
- 2 tbsp vinegar
- 2 tbsp grainy mustard
- 2 tbsp Dijon mustard
- ¼ cup honey
- Pepper
- Salt

Directions:

1. Place pork chops and remaining ingredients into the zip-lock bag, seal bag, and place in the refrigerator for overnight.
2. Preheat the grill over medium heat.
3. Place pork chops on the grill and cook for 3-5 minutes on each side.
4. Serve and enjoy.

Nutritional Value (Amount per Serving):

- Calories 337
- Fat 20.5 g
- Carbohydrates 19.2 g
- Sugar 17.6 g
- Protein 19 g
- Cholesterol 69 mg

Bourbon Pork Tenderloin

Preparation Time: 10 minutes
Cooking Time: 15 minutes
Serve: 6

Ingredients:

- 2 lbs pork tenderloins
- ¼ tsp garlic powder
- 1 lemon juice
- 2 tbsp Worcestershire sauce
- ¼ cup soy sauce
- ¼ cup brown sugar
- ½ cup bourbon

Directions:

1. Add pork tenderloins and remaining ingredients into the zip-lock bag. Seal bag and place in the refrigerator for overnight.
2. Preheat the grill over medium heat.
3. Place tenderloins on the grill and cook until the internal temperature reaches 145 F.
4. Serve and enjoy.

Nutritional Value (Amount per Serving):

- Calories 383
- Fat 12.3 g
- Carbohydrates 8 g
- Sugar 7.2 g
- Protein 45.9 g
- Cholesterol 142 mg

Juicy Pork Skewers

Preparation Time: 10 minutes
Cooking Time: 10 minutes
Serve: 10

Ingredients:

- 4 lbs pork shoulder, boneless & cut into chunks
- 1 cup mayonnaise
- ½ cup red wine
- 1 onion, grated
- 6 garlic cloves, minced
- 2 bell pepper, cut into chunks
- Pepper
- Salt

Directions:

1. Add pork chunks, mayonnaise, wine, onion, garlic, pepper, and salt into the mixing bowl and mix well. Cover and place in the refrigerator overnight.
2. Thread marinated pork chunks and bell pepper onto the skewers.
3. Preheat the grill over medium heat.
4. Place skewers on grill and cooks for 8-10 minutes or until internal temperature reaches 145 F.
5. Serve and enjoy.

Nutritional Value (Amount per Serving):

- Calories 646
- Fat 46.7 g
- Carbohydrates 9.4 g
- Sugar 3.3 g
- Protein 42.9 g
- Cholesterol 169 mg

Delicious Pork Patties

Preparation Time: 10 minutes
Cooking Time: 12 minutes
Serve: 4

Ingredients:

- 1 lb ground pork
- 1 cup carrot, shredded
- 1 tbsp rice vinegar
- 1 lb ground pork
- 2 tsp sesame oil
- 1 tbsp ginger, minced
- 2 garlic cloves, minced
- 2 scallions, chopped
- Pepper
- Salt

Directions:

1. Add all ingredients into the bowl and mix until well combined.
2. Make patties from the mixture.
3. Preheat the grill over medium heat.
4. Place patties on the grill and cook for 4-5 minutes or until internal temperature reaches to 155 F.
5. Serve and enjoy.

Nutritional Value (Amount per Serving):

- Calories 368
- Fat 10.3 g
- Carbohydrates 4.7 g
- Sugar 1.6 g
- Protein 60 g
- Cholesterol 166 mg

Lamb Loin Chops

Preparation Time: 10 minutes
Cooking Time: 10 minutes
Serve: 6

Ingredients:

- 12 lamb loin chops
- 2 tbsp rosemary, chopped
- 10 garlic cloves, chopped
- Pepper
- Salt

Directions:

1. Add lamb chops, rosemary, garlic, pepper, and salt into the mixing bowl and mix well. Cover and place in the refrigerator for 6 hours.
2. Preheat the grill over medium heat.
3. Brush grill grates with oil.
4. Place lamb chops on the grill and cook for 8-10 minutes or until the internal temperature reaches 130 F.
5. Serve and enjoy.

Nutritional Value (Amount per Serving):

- Calories 327
- Fat 12.7 g
- Carbohydrates 2.4 g
- Sugar 0.1 g
- Protein 48.1 g
- Cholesterol 153 mg

Greek Lamb Chops

Preparation Time: 10 minutes
Cooking Time: 10 minutes
Serve: 4

Ingredients:

- 1 ½ lbs lamb chops
- 2 tsp oregano
- 1 tbsp garlic, chopped
- 1 tbsp yogurt
- 1 lemon juice
- ¼ cup olive oil
- ¼ tsp pepper
- ¼ tsp salt

Directions:

1. Add all ingredients into the zip-lock bag. Seal bag and place in the refrigerator for overnight.
2. Preheat the grill over medium heat.
3. Place lamb chops on the grill and cook for 4-5 minutes on each side or until cooked through.
4. Serve and enjoy.

Nutritional Value (Amount per Serving):

- Calories 436
- Fat 25.3 g
- Carbohydrates 1.8 g
- Sugar 0.6 g
- Protein 48.3 g
- Cholesterol 153 mg

Classic Beef Patties

Preparation Time: 10 minutes
Cooking Time: 10 minutes
Serve: 8

Ingredients:

- 2 lbs ground beef
- 1 tsp dry mustard
- 1 tbsp paprika
- 2 tbsp granulated garlic
- ¼ cup brown sugar
- Pepper
- Salt

Directions:

1. Add all ingredients into the bowl and mix until well combined.
2. Preheat the grill over medium heat.
3. Make patties from mixture and place on grill and cook for 5 minutes on each side or until internal temperature reaches 165 F.
4. Serve and enjoy.

Nutritional Value (Amount per Serving):

- Calories 239
- Fat 7.3 g
- Carbohydrates 6.6 g
- Sugar 5 g
- Protein 35 g
- Cholesterol 101 mg

Flavorful Lamb Chops

Preparation Time: 10 minutes
Cooking Time: 12 minutes
Serve: 4

Ingredients:

- 8 lamb chops
- 2 tbsp harissa
- ½ tsp ground cumin
- 1 tbsp garlic, minced
- 2 tbsp lemon juice
- Pepper
- Salt

Directions:

1. Add lamb chops and remaining ingredients into the bowl and mix well. Cover and marinate for 1 hour.
2. Preheat the grill over medium heat.
3. Place lamb chops on the grill and cook for 4-6 minutes or until the internal temperature reaches 145 F.
4. Serve and enjoy.

Nutritional Value (Amount per Serving):

- Calories 347
- Fat 13.8 g
- Carbohydrates 4 g
- Sugar 2.2 g
- Protein 48.5 g
- Cholesterol 156 mg

Tandoori Lamb Chops

Preparation Time: 10 minutes
Cooking Time: 6 minutes
Serve: 2

Ingredients:

- 6 lamb chops
- ¼ tsp cayenne
- 2 tsp paprika
- 2 tbsp lemon juice
- 1 tsp ginger, minced
- 1 tsp garlic, minced
- 1 tbsp turmeric
- 1 ½ tbsp garam masala
- ¾ cup yogurt
- 1 tsp salt

Directions:

1. Add lamb chops and remaining ingredients into the bowl and mix well. Cover and place in the refrigerator for 1 hour.
2. Preheat the grill over medium heat.
3. Place lamb chops on the grill and cook for 2-3 minutes on each side or until cooked through.
4. Serve and enjoy.

Nutritional Value (Amount per Serving):

- Calories 567
- Fat 20.6 g
- Carbohydrates 11.4 g
- Sugar 7.2 g
- Protein 77.8 g
- Cholesterol 235 mg

Herb Lamb Skewers

Preparation Time: 10 minutes
Cooking Time: 10 minutes
Serve: 6

Ingredients:

- 1 ½ lbs lamb, cut into chunks
- ¼ cup olive oil
- 1/8 tsp chili flakes
- 1 lemon zest
- ½ tsp pepper
- 1 tbsp garlic, minced
- 2 tsp oregano, chopped
- 1 ½ tbsp parsley, chopped
- 1 ½ tbsp mint, chopped
- 1 ½ tbsp rosemary, chopped
- Pepper
- Salt

Directions:

1. Add lamb chunks and remaining ingredients into the bowl and mix well. Cover and place in the refrigerator overnight.
2. Preheat the grill over medium heat.
3. Thread marinated lamb chunks onto the skewers.
4. Place lamb skewers on grill and cook for 8-10 minutes or until cooked through.
5. Serve and enjoy.

Nutritional Value (Amount per Serving):

- Calories 294
- Fat 17 g
- Carbohydrates 2.5 g
- Sugar 0.3 g
- Protein 32.2 g
- Cholesterol 102 mg

Greek Lamb Patties

Preparation Time: 10 minutes
Cooking Time: 8 minutes
Serve: 4

Ingredients:

- 1 lb ground lamb
- 1 cup feta cheese, crumbled
- 1 tbsp garlic, minced
- 1 jalapeno pepper, minced
- 6 fresh basil leaves, chopped
- 10 mint leaves, chopped
- 1 tsp dried oregano
- Pepper
- Salt

Directions:

1. Add all ingredients into the bowl and mix until well combined.
2. Preheat the grill over medium heat.
3. Make patties from mixture and place on grill and cook for 4 minutes on each side.
4. Serve and enjoy.

Nutritional Value (Amount per Serving):

- Calories 328
- Fat 16.6 g
- Carbohydrates 5.1 g
- Sugar 1.7 g
- Protein 38.4 g
- Cholesterol 135 mg

Chapter 4: Fish & Seafood

Healthy Salmon Patties

Preparation Time: 10 minutes
Cooking Time: 8 minutes
Serve: 6

Ingredients:

- 2 eggs
- 1 lb salmon fillet
- 1 tbsp fresh lemon juice
- 1/4 cup mayonnaise
- 1 cup breadcrumbs
- 1 tsp mustard
- Pepper
- Salt

Directions:

1. Add all ingredients into the bowl and mix until well combined.
2. Make patties from the mixture.
3. Preheat the grill over medium heat.
4. Place patties on the grill and cook for 4 minutes on each side.
5. Serve and enjoy.

Nutritional Value (Amount per Serving):

- Calories 234
- Fat 10.5 g
- Carbohydrates 15.7 g
- Sugar 2 g
- Protein 19.2 g
- Cholesterol 90 mg

Lemon Pepper Salmon

Preparation Time: 10 minutes
Cooking Time: 8 minutes
Serve: 4

Ingredients:

- 1 lb salmon fillets
- 1/4 cup olive oil
- 1 lemon juice
- 1/2 tsp pepper
- 1 tsp sea salt

Directions:

1. In a large bowl, mix oil, lemon juice, pepper, and salt. Add salmon fillets and coat well. Cover and place in the refrigerator for 20 minutes.
2. Preheat the grill over medium heat.
3. Place salmon fillets on the grill and cook for 4 minutes on each side or until cooked.
4. Serve and enjoy.

Nutritional Value (Amount per Serving):

- Calories 261
- Fat 19.7 g
- Carbohydrates 0.4 g
- Sugar 0.3 g
- Protein 22.1 g
- Cholesterol 50 mg

Grilled Mahi Mahi

Preparation Time: 10 minutes
Cooking Time: 10 minutes
Serve: 2

Ingredients:

- 2 mahi-mahi fillets
- 2 tbsp fresh lemon juice
- 1 tsp cumin
- 1/2 tsp garlic powder
- 2 tbsp olive oil
- Pepper
- Salt

Directions:

1. In a small bowl, mix cumin, garlic powder, pepper, and salt.
2. Brush fish fillets with oil and season with spice mixture.
3. Preheat the grill over medium heat.
4. Place fish fillets on the grill and cook for 5 minutes on each side.
5. Drizzle with lemon juice and serve.

Nutritional Value (Amount per Serving):

- Calories 220
- Fat 15.4 g
- Carbohydrates 1.3 g
- Sugar 0.5 g
- Protein 30.4 g
- Cholesterol 80 mg

Blackened White Fish

Preparation Time: 10 minutes
Cooking Time: 8 minutes
Serve: 4

Ingredients:

- 4 white fish fillets
- 1 1/2 tbsp blackened seasoning
- 1 tbsp olive oil
- 1/2 tsp kosher salt

Directions:

1. Brush fish fillets with oil and sprinkle with blackened seasoning and salt.
2. Preheat the grill over medium heat.
3. Place fish fillets on the grill and cook for 4 minutes on each side.
4. Serve and enjoy.

Nutritional Value (Amount per Serving):

- Calories 295
- Fat 15.1 g
- Carbohydrates 0 g
- Sugar 0 g
- Protein 37.7 g
- Cholesterol 119 mg

Tasty Fish Skewers

Preparation Time: 10 minutes
Cooking Time: 10 minutes
Serve: 4

Ingredients:

- 1 1/2 lbs codfish fillets, cut into chunks
- 2 tbsp fresh lemon juice
- 4 garlic cloves, minced
- 2 bell peppers, cut into 1-inch pieces
- 1/2 tsp paprika
- 4 tbsp olive oil
- 1/4 tsp pepper
- 1 tsp kosher salt

Directions:

1. Add all ingredients into the mixing bowl and let it marinate for 1 hour.
2. Preheat the grill over medium heat.
3. Thread marinated fish chunks onto the skewers.
4. Place skewers on the grill and cook for 2-3 minutes on each side.
5. Serve and enjoy.

Nutritional Value (Amount per Serving):

- Calories 325
- Fat 15.7 g
- Carbohydrates 5.9 g
- Sugar 3.2 g
- Protein 39.7 g
- Cholesterol 94 mg

Spicy Salmon Fillets

Preparation Time: 10 minutes
Cooking Time: 10 minutes
Serve: 2

Ingredients:

- 2 salmon fillets
- 1 tbsp garlic, minced
- 1 jalapeno pepper, diced
- 2 tbsp lemon juice
- 3 tbsp mustard
- 1/4 cup olive oil
- 2 tbsp honey

Directions:

1. Add fish fillets and remaining ingredients into the zip-lock bag. Seal bag and place in the refrigerator for 30 minutes.
2. Preheat the grill over medium heat.
3. Place salmon fillets on the grill and cook for 5 minutes on each side.
4. Serve and enjoy.

Nutritional Value (Amount per Serving):

- Calories 606
- Fat 41.2 g
- Carbohydrates 25.3 g
- Sugar 19 g
- Protein 39.3 g
- Cholesterol 78 mg

Spicy White Fillets

Preparation Time: 10 minutes
Cooking Time: 10 minutes
Serve: 4

Ingredients:

- 2 lbs white fillets
- 1 tbsp garlic, minced
- 4 tbsp butter
- 1 tbsp fresh lemon juice
- 3 tbsp olive oil
- 1/4 tsp cayenne
- 2 tbsp fresh basil, chopped

Directions:

1. Add fish fillets, lemon juice, and oil into the bowl and mix well. Cover and set aside for 30 minutes.
2. Preheat the grill over medium heat.
3. Place fish fillets on the grill and cook for 5 minutes on each side.
4. Serve and enjoy.

Nutritional Value (Amount per Serving):

- Calories 371
- Fat 30.9 g
- Carbohydrates 12 g
- Sugar 2.2 g
- Protein 17.3 g
- Cholesterol 31 mg

Greek Fish Fillets

Preparation Time: 10 minutes
Cooking Time: 10 minutes
Serve: 4

Ingredients:

- 4 cod fish fillets

For marinade:

- 1 1/2 tsp dried basil
- 2 tbsp lemon juice
- 6 tbsp olive oil
- 1 tbsp garlic paste
- 1 tsp spike seasoning
- 1 tsp pepper

Directions:

1. Add fish fillets and all marinade ingredients into the zip-lock bag. Seal bag and place in the refrigerator for 30 minutes.
2. Preheat the grill over medium heat.
3. Place fish fillets on the grill and cook for 5 minutes on each side.
4. Serve and enjoy.

Nutritional Value (Amount per Serving):

- Calories 375
- Fat 22.6 g
- Carbohydrates 1.2 g
- Sugar 0.2 g
- Protein 41.4 g
- Cholesterol 99 mg

Asian Fish Fillets

Preparation Time: 10 minutes
Cooking Time: 10 minutes
Serve: 5

Ingredients:

- 1 1/2 lbs white fish fillets
- 1 tbsp fish sauce
- 1 tbsp olive oil
- 1/4 cup cilantro, chopped
- 2 tsp garlic, minced
- 2 lime juice
- 2 tsp soy sauce

Directions:

1. Add fish fillets and remaining ingredients into the zip-lock bag. Seal bag and place in the refrigerator for 30 minutes.
2. Preheat the grill over medium heat.
3. Place fish fillets on the grill and cook for 5 minutes on each side.
4. Serve and enjoy.

Nutritional Value (Amount per Serving):

- Calories 267
- Fat 13 g
- Carbohydrates 2.2 g
- Sugar 0.5 g
- Protein 33.8 g
- Cholesterol 105 mg

Quick Shrimp Skewers

Preparation Time: 10 minutes
Cooking Time: 6 minutes
Serve: 4

Ingredients:

- 1 1/2 lbs shrimp, peeled & deveined
- 1 tbsp chili powder
- 1 tbsp lime juice
- 2 tbsp olive oil
- 1 tsp kosher salt

Directions:

1. Add shrimp and remaining ingredients into the bowl and mix well.
2. Thread shrimp onto the skewers.
3. Preheat the grill over medium heat.
4. Place shrimp skewers on grill and cook for 2-3 minutes on each side.
5. Serve and enjoy.

Nutritional Value (Amount per Serving):

- Calories 271
- Fat 10.2 g
- Carbohydrates 4.5 g
- Sugar 0.3 g
- Protein 39 g
- Cholesterol 358 mg

Lime Butter Fish Fillets

Preparation Time: 10 minutes
Cooking Time: 12 minutes
Serve: 4

Ingredients:

- 1 1/2 lbs cod fish fillets
- 2 tbsp butter, melted
- 1 lime zest
- 2 tbsp lime juice
- Pepper
- Salt

Directions:

1. In a small bowl, mix butter, lime juice, lime zest, pepper, and salt.
2. Preheat the grill over medium heat.
3. Brush fish fillets with butter mixture and place on grill and cook for 5-6 minutes on each side.
4. Serve and enjoy.

Nutritional Value (Amount per Serving):

- Calories 235
- Fat 7.2 g
- Carbohydrates 2 g
- Sugar 0.4 g
- Protein 39 g
- Cholesterol 109 mg

Delicious Swordfish

Preparation Time: 10 minutes
Cooking Time: 10 minutes
Serve: 4

Ingredients:

- 4 swordfish steaks
- 1 1/2 tbsp honey
- 1/4 cup olive oil
- 1/4 tsp pepper
- 3/4 tsp garlic, minced
- 1 1/2 tbsp soy sauce
- 1/2 tsp kosher salt

Directions:

1. Add swordfish and remaining ingredients into the zip-lock bag. Seal bag and place in the refrigerator for 5 hours.
2. Preheat the grill over medium heat.
3. Place fish fillets on the grill and cook for 5 minutes on each side.
4. Serve and enjoy.

Nutritional Value (Amount per Serving):

- Calories 301
- Fat 18.1 g
- Carbohydrates 7.2 g
- Sugar 6.6 g
- Protein 27.4 g
- Cholesterol 53 mg

Marinated Shrimp Skewers

Preparation Time: 10 minutes
Cooking Time: 6 minutes
Serve: 8

Ingredients:

- 1 lb shrimp, peeled & deveined

For marinade:

- 2 garlic cloves, minced
- 1/2 cup orange juice
- 1/4 cup olive oil
- 2 tbsp Sriracha
- 1 lime juice
- 1/2 tsp kosher salt

Directions:

1. Add shrimp and all marinade ingredients into the zip-lock bag. Seal bag and place in the refrigerator for 30 minutes.
2. Thread shrimp onto the skewers.
3. Preheat the grill over medium heat.
4. Place skewers on the grill and cook for 3 minutes on each side.
5. Serve and enjoy.

Nutritional Value (Amount per Serving):

- Calories 135
- Fat 7.3 g
- Carbohydrates 3.8 g
- Sugar 1.4 g
- Protein 13.1 g
- Cholesterol 119 mg

Easy Grill Scallops

Preparation Time: 10 minutes
Cooking Time: 6 minutes
Serve: 4

Ingredients:

- 1 lb sea scallops
- 1 tbsp fresh lemon juice
- 2 tbsp butter, melted
- Pepper
- Salt

Directions:

1. Add scallop and remaining ingredients into a bowl and mix well.
2. Preheat the grill over medium heat.
3. Place scallops on grill and cooks for 2-3 minutes on each side.
4. Serve and enjoy.

Nutritional Value (Amount per Serving):

- Calories 152
- Fat 6.7 g
- Carbohydrates 2.8 g
- Sugar 0.1 g
- Protein 19.1 g
- Cholesterol 53 mg

Blackened Haddock

Preparation Time: 10 minutes
Cooking Time: 8 minutes
Serve: 4

Ingredients:

- 4 haddock fish fillets
- 2 tbsp blackened seasoning
- 1 tbsp olive oil
- 1/2 tsp kosher salt

Directions:

1. Brush fish fillets with oil and sprinkle with blackened seasoning and salt.
2. Preheat the grill over medium heat.
3. place fish fillets on the grill and cook for 4 minutes on each side or until internal temperature reaches 130 F.
4. Serve and enjoy.

Nutritional Value (Amount per Serving):

- Calories 186
- Fat 5 g
- Carbohydrates 2.3 g
- Sugar 0.1 g
- Protein 32.4 g
- Cholesterol 82 mg

Chapter 5: Vegetables & Side Dishes

Perfect Brussels Sprouts

Preparation Time: 10 minutes
Cooking Time: 15 minutes
Serve: 6

Ingredients:

- 1 ½ lbs Brussels sprouts, cut in half
- 1 tsp garlic, minced
- 1 ½ tsp Italian seasoning
- ¼ tsp pepper
- 1 tbsp lemon juice
- 4 tbsp olive oil
- Pepper
- Salt

Directions:

1. Add Brussels sprouts and remaining ingredients into the bowl and mix well. Cover and set aside for 30 minutes.
2. Preheat the grill over medium heat.
3. Thread Brussels sprouts onto the skewers.
4. Place skewers on the grill and cook for 3-4 minutes on each side.
5. Serve and enjoy.

Nutritional Value (Amount per Serving):

- Calories 134
- Fat 10.1 g
- Carbohydrates 10.7 g
- Sugar 2.6 g
- Protein 3.9 g
- Cholesterol 1 mg

Tender Asparagus

Preparation Time: 10 minutes
Cooking Time: 10 minutes
Serve: 4

Ingredients:

- 1 lb asparagus spears
- 1 tbsp olive oil
- Pepper
- Salt

Directions:

1. Brush asparagus spears with oil and season with pepper and salt.
2. Preheat the grill over medium heat.
3. Place asparagus spears on grill and cook for 6-10 minutes.
4. Serve and enjoy.

Nutritional Value (Amount per Serving):

- Calories 53
- Fat 3.6 g
- Carbohydrates 4.4 g
- Sugar 2.1 g
- Protein 2.5 g
- Cholesterol 0 mg

Grill Garlic Zucchini

Preparation Time: 10 minutes
Cooking Time: 10 minutes
Serve: 4

Ingredients:

- 2 zucchini, cut into ½-inch slices
- 1 tbsp tomato sauce
- 2 tsp soy sauce
- 2 garlic cloves, minced
- 2 tbsp olive oil
- Pepper
- Salt

Directions:

1. Add zucchini and remaining ingredients into the bowl and mix well.
2. Preheat the grill over medium heat.
3. Place zucchini slices on grill and cook for 2-3 minutes on each side.
4. Serve and enjoy.

Nutritional Value (Amount per Serving):

- Calories 80
- Fat 7.2 g
- Carbohydrates 4.2 g
- Sugar 1.9 g
- Protein 1.5 g
- Cholesterol 0 mg

Flavorful Grill Eggplant

Preparation Time: 10 minutes
Cooking Time: 15 minutes
Serve: 6

Ingredients:

- 2 large eggplants, cut into ½-inch thick slices
- 1 ½ tsp garlic, minced
- 1 ½ tsp Italian seasoning
- 2 tbsp lemon juice
- 5 tbsp olive oil
- Pepper
- Salt

Directions:

1. Add eggplant slices and remaining ingredients into the bowl and mix well. Cover and set aside for 2 hours.
2. Preheat the grill over medium heat.
3. Place eggplant slices on grill and cook for 3-4 minutes on each side.
4. Serve and enjoy.

Nutritional Value (Amount per Serving):

- Calories 152
- Fat 12.4 g
- Carbohydrates 11.2 g
- Sugar 5.7 g
- Protein 1.9 g
- Cholesterol 1 mg

Simple Grill Sweet Potatoes

Preparation Time: 10 minutes
Cooking Time: 10 minutes
Serve: 4

Ingredients:

- 2 lbs sweet potatoes, cut into ½-inch thick slices
- 3 tbsp olive oil
- Pepper
- Salt

Directions:

1. Add sweet potato slices, oil, pepper, and salt into the bowl and mix well.
2. Preheat the grill over medium heat.
3. Place sweet potato slices on the grill and cook for 5 minutes on each side.
4. Serve and enjoy.

Nutritional Value (Amount per Serving):

- Calories 286
- Fat 8.7 g
- Carbohydrates 50.6 g
- Sugar 0.9 g
- Protein 2.8 g
- Cholesterol 0 mg

Balsamic Vegetables

Preparation Time: 10 minutes
Cooking Time: 10 minutes
Serve: 4

Ingredients:

- 1 small zucchini, cut into ½-inch thick slices
- 1 cup cherry tomatoes
- 8 oz mushrooms, halved
- 1 bell pepper, cut into chunks
- 1 onion, cut into chunks
- 1 tbsp rosemary, chopped
- 1 garlic clove, minced
- 2 tsp balsamic vinegar
- 2 tbsp olive oil
- Pepper
- Salt

Directions:

1. Add all ingredients into the bowl and mix well and set aside for 30 minutes.
2. Preheat the grill over medium heat.
3. Thread vegetable pieces onto the skewers.
4. Place skewers on grill and cooks for 8-12 minutes or until cooked.
5. Serve and enjoy.

Nutritional Value (Amount per Serving):

- Calories 110
- Fat 7.5 g
- Carbohydrates 10.2 g
- Sugar 5.4 g
- Protein 3.2 g
- Cholesterol 0 mg

Grill Mushrooms & Zucchini

Preparation Time: 10 minutes
Cooking Time: 15 minutes
Serve: 8

Ingredients:

- 2 lbs mushrooms
- 4 small zucchini, sliced
- 2 tbsp olive oil
- Salt

Directions:

1. Add mushrooms, zucchini slices, oil, and salt into the bowl and mix well.
2. Preheat the grill over medium heat.
3. Place vegetables on the grill and cook for 5-6 minutes on each side.
4. Serve and enjoy.

Nutritional Value (Amount per Serving):

- Calories 64
- Fat 3.9 g
- Carbohydrates 5.7 g
- Sugar 3 g
- Protein 4.3 g
- Cholesterol 0 mg

Grill Carrots

Preparation Time: 10 minutes
Cooking Time: 12 minutes
Serve: 6

Ingredients:

- 12 carrots, peel
- ½ tsp thyme
- ½ tsp rosemary
- 3 tbsp olive oil
- Pepper
- Salt

Directions:

1. Add carrots and remaining ingredients into the bowl and mix well.
2. Preheat the grill over medium heat.
3. Place carrots on the grill and cook for 10-12 minutes.
4. Serve and enjoy.

Nutritional Value (Amount per Serving):

- Calories 111
- Fat 7 g
- Carbohydrates 12.1 g
- Sugar 6 g
- Protein 1 g
- Cholesterol 0 mg

Grill Tomatoes

Preparation Time: 10 minutes
Cooking Time: 4 minutes
Serve: 2

Ingredients:

- 2 tomatoes, cut in half
- Pepper
- Salt

Directions:

1. Preheat the grill over medium heat.
2. Place tomatoes cut side down on the grill and cook for 4 minutes.
3. Serve and enjoy.

Nutritional Value (Amount per Serving):

- Calories 22
- Fat 0.3 g
- Carbohydrates 4.8 g
- Sugar 3.2 g
- Protein 1.1 g
- Cholesterol 0 mg

Grill Avocado

Preparation Time: 10 minutes
Cooking Time: 5 minutes
Serve: 6

Ingredients:

- 3 avocados, cut in half & remove the pit
- Pepper
- Salt

Directions:

1. Preheat the grill over medium heat.
2. Season avocado with pepper and salt and place cut side down on the grill and cook for 5 minutes.
3. Serve and enjoy.

Nutritional Value (Amount per Serving):

- Calories 205
- Fat 19.6 g
- Carbohydrates 8.7 g
- Sugar 0.5 g
- Protein 1.9 g
- Cholesterol 0 mg

Chapter 6: Snacks

Chili Lime Shrimp Skewers

Preparation Time: 10 minutes
Cooking Time: 6 minutes
Serve: 4

Ingredients:

- 12 shrimp
- 1 cup pineapple chunks
- ¼ cup honey
- 1 tsp chili sauce
- 2 tbsp olive oil
- Pepper
- Salt

Directions:

1. Add shrimp and remaining ingredients into the bowl and mix well. Cover and set aside for 30 minutes.
2. Preheat the grill over medium heat.
3. Thread shrimp and pineapple pieces onto the skewers.
4. Place skewers on the grill and cook for 3 minutes on each side.
5. Serve and enjoy.

Nutritional Value (Amount per Serving):

- Calories 224
- Fat 8.2 g
- Carbohydrates 23.9 g
- Sugar 21.5 g
- Protein 15.3 g
- Cholesterol 139 mg

Tofu Steaks

Preparation Time: 10 minutes
Cooking Time: 14 minutes
Serve: 4

Ingredients:

- 14 oz extra-firm tofu, pressed & cut into slices
- 1 tbsp olive oil
- ¾ cup BBQ sauce

Directions:

1. Add tofu slices, oil, and BBQ sauce into the bowl and mix well.
2. Preheat the grill over medium heat.
3. Place tofu slices on grill and cook for 7 minutes on each side.
4. Serve and enjoy.

Nutritional Value (Amount per Serving):

- Calories 191
- Fat 9.4 g
- Carbohydrates 19 g
- Sugar 12.7 g
- Protein 9.8 g
- Cholesterol 0 mg

Pineapple Shrimp Skewers

Preparation Time: 10 minutes
Cooking Time: 6 minutes
Serve: 4

Ingredients:

- 18 shrimp
- 1 tsp dried oregano
- 2 tbsp butter, melted
- 1 ½ cups pineapple chunks
- ¾ tsp sea salt

Directions:

1. Add shrimp, oregano, butter, pineapple, and salt into the bowl and mix well.
2. Preheat the grill over medium heat.
3. Thread pineapple pieces and shrimp onto the skewers.
4. Place skewers on the grill and cook for 3 minutes on each side.
5. Serve and enjoy.

Nutritional Value (Amount per Serving):

- Calories 200
- Fat 7.6 g
- Carbohydrates 9.9 g
- Sugar 6.1 g
- Protein 23 g
- Cholesterol 224 mg

Spicy Tofu Skewers

Preparation Time: 10 minutes
Cooking Time: 10 minutes
Serve: 8

Ingredients:

- 1 package extra-firm tofu, pressed & cut into cubes
- 1 tbsp olive oil
- 1 tsp rice vinegar
- 2 tsp sriracha
- ½ tsp garlic powder
- ½ tbsp maple syrup
- 2 tbsp soy sauce

Directions:

1. Add tofu and remaining ingredients into the bowl and mix well.
2. Preheat the grill over medium heat.
3. Thread tofu pieces onto the skewers.
4. Place skewers on the grill and cook for 5 minutes on each side.
5. Serve and enjoy.

Nutritional Value (Amount per Serving):

- Calories 33
- Fat 2.4 g
- Carbohydrates 1.8 g
- Sugar 0.9 g
- Protein 1.4 g
- Cholesterol 0 mg

Mushroom Skewers

Preparation Time: 10 minutes
Cooking Time: 16 minutes
Serve: 4

Ingredients:

- 1 ½ lbs mushrooms
- 2 tsp thyme, chopped
- 1 ½ tbsp soy sauce
- 1 tbsp garlic, minced
- ¼ cup butter, melted
- Salt

Directions:

1. Add mushroom and remaining ingredients into the bowl and mix well.
2. Preheat the grill over medium heat.
3. Thread mushrooms onto the skewers.
4. Place skewers on the grill and cooks for 8 minutes on each side.
5. Serve and enjoy.

Nutritional Value (Amount per Serving):

- Calories 146
- Fat 12.1 g
- Carbohydrates 7.1 g
- Sugar 3.1 g
- Protein 6 g
- Cholesterol 31 mg

Pineapple Chicken Skewers

Preparation Time: 10 minutes
Cooking Time: 12 minutes
Serve: 6

Ingredients:

- 2 lbs chicken breasts, boneless & cut into chunks
- 1 cup pineapple juice
- 1 pineapple, cut into chunks
- 1 tsp ginger, grated
- 1 tsp garlic, minced
- 2 tbsp Dijon mustard
- 1/3 cup soy sauce
- ½ cup brown sugar

Directions:

1. Add chicken, pineapple juice, pineapple chunks, ginger, garlic, mustard, soy sauce, and brown sugar into the bowl and mix well. Cover and place in the refrigerator for 6 hours.
2. Preheat the grill over medium heat.
3. Thread pineapple and chicken onto the skewers.
4. Place skewers on the grill and cooks for 6 minutes on each side.
5. Serve and enjoy.

Nutritional Value (Amount per Serving):

- Calories 382
- Fat 11.5 g
- Carbohydrates 22.6 g
- Sugar 18.9 g
- Protein 45.2 g
- Cholesterol 135 mg

Hawaiian Chicken Skewers

Preparation Time: 10 minutes
Cooking Time: 10 minutes
Serve: 4

Ingredients:

- 1 ½ lbs chicken breasts, boneless & cut into chunks
- 1 pineapple, cut into chunks
- 2 bell peppers, cut into chunks
- 1 cup BBQ sauce
- 1 tsp garlic, minced
- 1 tsp ginger, minced
- 1 tbsp olive oil
- 1 tbsp soy sauce
- ¼ cup pineapple juice
- Pepper
- Salt

Directions:

1. Add all ingredients into the bowl and mix well. Cover and set aside for 4 hours.
2. Preheat the grill over medium heat.
3. Thread chicken, pineapple, and bell pepper pieces onto the skewers.
4. Place skewers on the grill and cook for 5 minutes on each side.
5. Serve and enjoy.

Nutritional Value (Amount per Serving):

- Calories 500
- Fat 16.5 g
- Carbohydrates 35.5 g
- Sugar 25 g
- Protein 50.4 g
- Cholesterol 151 mg

Simple Chicken Skewers

Preparation Time: 10 minutes
Cooking Time: 16 minutes
Serve: 4

Ingredients:

- 1 lb chicken breasts, boneless & cut into chunks
- 1 lemon juice
- 3 tbsp Greek seasoning
- 1 tbsp garlic, minced
- 1 tbsp vinegar
- 2 tbsp olive oil
- Pepper
- Salt

Directions:

1. Add chicken and remaining ingredients into the bowl and mix well and allow to marinate for 4 hours.
2. Preheat the grill over medium heat.
3. Thread chicken pieces onto the skewers.
4. Place skewers on the grill and cooks for 8 minutes on each side.
5. Serve and enjoy.

Nutritional Value (Amount per Serving):

- Calories 298
- Fat 15.7 g
- Carbohydrates 4.4 g
- Sugar 0.3 g
- Protein 33.5 g
- Cholesterol 101 mg

Mexican Grill Shrimp

Preparation Time: 10 minutes
Cooking Time: 6 minutes
Serve: 4

Ingredients:

- 1 lb shrimp, peel & deveined
- 1 tsp cumin
- 1 tsp onion powder
- 1 tsp garlic powder
- 1 tsp chili powder
- 1 tsp smoked paprika
- 1 tbsp brown sugar
- 1 tsp jalapeno, minced
- 1 tsp garlic, chopped
- 1/3 cup olive oil
- 1 tsp kosher salt

Directions:

1. Add shrimp and remaining ingredients into the bowl and mix well and allow to marinate for 4 hours.
2. Preheat the grill over medium heat.
3. Thread shrimp onto the skewers.
4. Place skewers on the grill and cook for 3 minutes on each side.
5. Serve and enjoy.

Nutritional Value (Amount per Serving):

- Calories 298
- Fat 19 g
- Carbohydrates 6.1 g
- Sugar 2.7 g
- Protein 26.3 g
- Cholesterol 239 mg

Grill Pork Patties

Preparation Time: 10 minutes
Cooking Time: 10 minutes
Serve: 4

Ingredients:

- 1 lb ground pork
- 1 tbsp olive oil
- ¼ tsp dried thyme
- ½ tsp ground coriander
- ½ tsp smoked paprika
- ½ tsp pepper
- ½ tsp fennel seeds
- ½ tsp chili flakes
- Pepper
- Salt

Directions:

1. Add all ingredients into the bowl and mix until well combined.
2. Preheat the grill over medium heat.
3. Make patties from mixture and place on grill and cook for 5 minutes on each side.
4. Serve and enjoy.

Nutritional Value (Amount per Serving):

- Calories 195
- Fat 7.6 g
- Carbohydrates 0.5 g
- Sugar 0 g
- Protein 29.8 g
- Cholesterol 83 mg

Chapter 7: Desserts

Delicious Grill Pineapple

Preparation Time: 10 minutes
Cooking Time: 8 minutes
Serve: 8

Ingredients:

- 1 pineapple, cut into rings
- 2 tbsp brown sugar
- 1 tbsp honey
- ¼ cup butter, melted

Directions:

1. Add pineapple rings, brown sugar, honey, and butter into the zip-lock bag, seal bag, and place in the refrigerator for 30 minutes.
2. Preheat the grill over medium heat.
3. Place pineapple rings on the grill and cook for 6-8 minutes on each side.
4. Serve and enjoy.

Nutritional Value (Amount per Serving):

- Calories 78
- Fat 5.8 g
- Carbohydrates 7.1 g
- Sugar 6.4 g
- Protein 0.2 g
- Cholesterol 15 mg

Grill Apple Slices

Preparation Time: 10 minutes
Cooking Time: 12 minutes
Serve: 4

Ingredients:

- 3 apples, core & cut into ½-inch slices
- 1 tbsp butter, melted
- 1/3 cup brown sugar
- 2 tbsp honey
- ½ tsp cinnamon
- 2 tbsp olive oil
- 2 tbsp fresh lemon juice

Directions:

1. In a small bowl, mix butter, brown sugar, honey, cinnamon, oil, and lemon juice.
2. Brush apple slices with butter mixture.
3. Preheat the grill over medium heat.
4. Place apple slices on grill and cook for 4-6 minutes on each side.
5. Serve and enjoy.

Nutritional Value (Amount per Serving):

- Calories 253
- Fat 1.2 g
- Carbohydrates 44 g
- Sugar 37.9 g
- Protein 0.6 g
- Cholesterol 8 mg

Grilled Peaches

Preparation Time: 10 minutes
Cooking Time: 20 minutes
Serve: 4

Ingredients:

- 4 peaches, cut in half
- ¼ cup pecans, toasted
- 1 tbsp butter, melted
- 3 tbsp honey
- ¼ cup brown sugar

Directions:

1. In a small bowl, mix honey and brown sugar. Set aside.
2. Preheat the grill over medium heat.
3. Brush peaches with butter and place on cut side on grill and cook for 5 minutes.
4. Flip peaches and top with honey sugar mixture and grill for 10-15 minutes more.
5. Sprinkle with pecans and serve.

Nutritional Value (Amount per Serving):

- Calories 58
- Fat 1.3 g
- Carbohydrates 12 g
- Sugar 11.9 g
- Protein 0.5 g
- Cholesterol 3 mg

Grill Pears

Preparation Time: 10 minutes
Cooking Time: 10 minutes
Serve: 4

Ingredients:

- 4 pears, cut in half, and scoop out seeds
- 2 tbsp brown sugar
- 1 tbsp butter, melted

Directions:

1. Brush pears with melted butter.
2. Preheat the grill over medium heat.
3. Place pears cut side down on the grill and cook for 10 minutes or until tender.
4. Sprinkle with brown sugar and serve.

Nutritional Value (Amount per Serving):

- Calories 163
- Fat 3.2 g
- Carbohydrates 36.2 g
- Sugar 24.8 g
- Protein 0.8 g
- Cholesterol 8 mg

Fruit Skewers

Preparation Time: 10 minutes
Cooking Time: 10 minutes
Serve: 4

Ingredients:

- 2 cups pineapple chunks
- 2 cups peaches, cut into chunks
- ¼ tsp cinnamon
- ¼ cup honey

Directions:

1. Add pineapple, peaches, cinnamon, and honey into the bowl and mix well.
2. Preheat the grill over medium heat.
3. Thread pineapple pieces and peach pieces onto the skewers.
4. Place fruit skewers on the grill and cook for 5 minutes on each side.
5. Serve and enjoy.

Nutritional Value (Amount per Serving):

- Calories 135
- Fat 0.3 g
- Carbohydrates 35.4 g
- Sugar 32.5 g
- Protein 1.2 g
- Cholesterol 0 mg

Conclusion

The Weber Spirit II is one of the innovative and advanced gas grills works on liquid propane gas. The grill comes with compact size and made up from stainless steel material. If you enjoy your weekends and holidays cooking outdoor food on regular basis then Weber spirit II gas grill is one of the best options available in the market which fulfils your outdoor cooking needs.

This cookbook contains 80 healthy and tasty recipes comes from different categories like poultry, beef, pork, lamb, seafood, fish, side dishes, vegetables, snacks, and desserts. The recipes written in this book are unique and written into an easily understandable form. All the recipes start with their preparation and cooking time followed by step by step cooking instructions. In the end, each recipe ends with their nutritional value information.

www.ingramcontent.com/pod-product-compliance
Lightning Source LLC
Chambersburg PA
CBHW082040080526
44578CB00009B/765